MW01166479

The
Privilege
of *Prayer*

Study Guide

Author: James P. Winsor

Editors: Thomas J. Doyle and Arnold E. Schmidt
Editorial Assistant: Marilyn Weber

Contents

The Privilege of Prayer

In the United States most people have access to a telephone. But sometimes the communication system breaks down because of ice storms, accidents, human error, or natural disasters. Communication stops. Telephone service personnel then have to repair the damage.

Once an intimate and personal relationship existed between people and their Creator. Then sin entered the world. As a result, communication with God was cut off, for fallen sinners were no longer on speaking terms with God. Communication stopped. Prayer was impossible.

Because people were neither willing nor able to repair the break, God sent His Son Jesus Christ. By obeying the Law on our behalf, by suffering, dying, and rising from the dead, our Lord restored the broken relationship that existed between us and God. Jesus did what we could never do for ourselves. God restored communication between Him and us. Now again we can communicate with God in prayer.

Thanks to the merits of Jesus Christ, we have open access to God. God invites us to come to Him directly, confidently, and boldly in our prayers. What a privilege is ours!

Lesson 1   Give Thanks:
The 10 Men with Leprosy

Luke 17:11–19

Our Itinerary

In this session we will explore how God's love for us motivates us to give Him thanks. We demonstrate our gratitude in prayer and worship. We will explore how our grateful worship is more than mere thoughts, words, and feelings. We will also share with one another the reasons we have to be grateful to God and ways we can express that gratitude.

Invited into the Adventure

Tim and Julie had begun their married life just as they had intended—regularly attending worship. As life-long Christians, they were grateful for each other, for each other's faith, and for their new life together. They wanted to offer their thanks and praise regularly. But more recently, things have taken a different turn.

Julie: Tim, do you realize this is the fourth weekend in a row you've worked on Saturday and played golf with the guys from the office on Sunday morning?

Tim: Has it really been four weekends? Well, you know I don't have much time lately.

Julie: Well, your co-worker, Akbar, seems to find the time to go to church. And he doesn't have a Christian family or background! I'm about ready to go to church without you. But I'd much rather not have to explain your absence.

Tim: Well, you know what they say, "If it works, don't fix it." And things finally seem to be working for us. This new job really pays well. We've almost paid off all the debts from when I was out of work. You can't expect the good accounts that I have received to be there if I don't put in the hours and play golf with the guys who control those accounts. You know that, honey. When things are working this well, I don't want to tinker with the dials. Do you know what I mean?

Julie: I think I do. I think you mean that you're not going to church because you're afraid you'll lose some good accounts and some good income.

5

Tim: Well, I wouldn't put it that way. What I'm really getting at is that I think God blesses us because we're doing what He wants; we're working hard and playing by the rules. And it's paying off. God respects hard work and rewards cleverness.

Julie: I'd say *we've* ignored Him.

Tim: No! We went to church just last month. Don't you remember? We even stayed after to ask God for some help with the job hunt. Don't you remember?

Julie: Yes! *Don't you?*

Let's Talk

1. Tim and Julie began their marriage with regular church attendance. What seems to have motivated that attendance? Share, if you wish, a time when you attended worship for the same reason. More recently Tim and Julie have stopped attending worship. Why has Tim stopped? Julie?

2. How do you know Akbar's behavior bothers Julie? Can you think of an "Akbar" in your life?

3. Review Julie's last line. What does she think should motivate Tim to attend worship? To what does Tim credit his success in business? How might this affect his interest in attending worship?

Grounds for Gratitude
Read **Luke 17:11–14.**

1. Jesus traveled along the border between Samaria and Galilee. Samaritan religion was based on a mixture of the Law of Moses and pagan religions. This sort of mixture had gotten Israel into serious trouble during the days of the prophets when God had punished Israel for not worshiping Him alone. Jewish people in Jesus' day would go a great distance out of their way rather than travel through Samaria. Given this background, why do you suppose devout Jews avoided Samaritans? What groups of people today might you compare to the Samaritans?

2. In **verse 16** we learn that at least one of the 10 men was a Samaritan. Here we find Jewish believers and a Samaritan in close friendly contact. Special needs and burdens often draw together people who would otherwise have nothing to do with one another.

a. Can you think of some recent events that have drawn people together?

b. How do trials and crises bring together people who would probably not associate with one another?

c. What does the relationship the Jewish men shared with the Samaritan tell us about these Jews?

d. What consequence of their skin disease is evident in this unique relationship between Jew and Samaritan?

3. Reread **verse 13.** The lepers' cry to Jesus is simple, direct, and strong. They say nothing to indicate that they feel they deserve His healing. They say nothing about their misery. They make no promise to pay Him back with an obedient life. They don't even lay their need before Him. They simply cry out from a distance, "Jesus, Master, have pity on us!"

a. How might our personal prayers sometimes differ from this simplicity and honesty?

b. How can this model prayer assist us to pray "without ceasing"?

c. If you wish, share a time when you prayed with this sort of desperate simplicity.

4. The prayer "Master, have pity on us" is the basis for the prayer "Lord, have mercy on us."

a. Think of some occasions where you have prayed or heard someone else pray, "Lord, have mercy on us."

b. Why is this an appropriate prayer for us to pray together while gathered for worship? at other times?

5. According to the law of Moses people healed of a skin disease were to present themselves to the priest for confirmation that the disease was gone **(Leviticus 13:16–17).** The priest, somewhat like a medical examiner, could remove the "unclean" label and give the go ahead for a person to reenter life in the community. Jesus sent these men to the priest before they were healed. While they were on the way, the disease left them.

a. Why do you think Jesus handled the situation in this way?

b. When might it be appropriate for us, having prayed for something, to go ahead and behave as if God's answer were a definite yes even though the answer has not been confirmed by experience?

c. Share a time when Jesus brought about healing as a response to your prayer or to that of another believer.

d. Beyond physical healing, what even greater healing has God provided for us? See **Psalm 103:1–3** for ideas.

6. Read **Matthew 8:14–17.** Now read **Isaiah 53:3–7.** When Jesus suffered and died on the cross, He did exactly what Isaiah predicted—He was "pierced for our transgressions." Jesus absorbed God's punishment for our sins into Himself so that we do not and will not receive angry punishment from God. Why might we speak of Jesus' death as His greatest healing work?

Hit the Ground in Gratitude

Read **Luke 17:15–19.**

1. Compare the man's proximity to Jesus now with his proximity earlier. Although the man spoke to Jesus before, he now draws physically close to Him.

a. Beyond the obvious—no longer considered contagious—what might also explain His closer proximity?

b. How does Jesus' healing of us enable us to draw near to Him?

2. Read **Hebrews 10:19–25.** The ark of the covenant dwelt in the Most Holy Place or the Holy of Holies. Here God's presence was recognized and assured. A thick embroidered curtain made this area inaccessible to the people. When Jesus died as the sacrifice for our sins, the curtain split. This signaled our direct access to God through Jesus' death.

a. What are some of the ways in which this passage of Scripture describes our condition as a result of Jesus' death for us?

b. How can we make use of the access Jesus won for us by healing us from the leprosy of sin **(Hebrews 13:15)**?

3. The Samaritan who returned to thank Jesus knew that Jesus was capable of receiving his thanks from a distance. After all, Jesus had healed the man from a distance. Yet the man returned *physically* and he *physically* threw himself at Jesus' feet. His disease had been *physical*. His healing was *physical*. His praise was *physical*.

Jesus, by enduring *physical* suffering and spiritual torment, saved us from spiritual and *physical* agony in hell **(Luke 16:22–24).** What does this suggest about how we might offer thanks to God? See **Philippians 2:9–11** and **1 Timothy 2:8–10** for additional ideas.

4. The Samaritan in our lesson was, as a Samaritan, the least likely to "do the right thing." But he was the only one who did that which Jesus deserved. Jesus' question remains unanswered, "Where are the other nine?" Perhaps they were more interested in sharing their excitement with family or friends or more interested in doing some of the social things that were out of reach prior to their healing. Perhaps they felt legally bound to go straight to the priests and not turn back, as if their walking had brought about and would preserve their healing. Scripture does not say. It is clear that the man who once had the greatest barrier returned to thank Jesus. How are we like him?

Grounded in a Grateful Eternity

Read **Revelation 7:9–14.** For what can we be thankful no matter how tough things may get? Name some things about heaven as it is described in these verses for which you can be thankful. What will our communication with God still include in heaven?

Venturing Out Together

1. Find hymns of thanks in the hymnal. Sing or read a few together.

2. Use markers or colored pencils to design a Bible bookmark that includes passages of thanks. Or design a bookmark with a short original prayer of thanksgiving. Consider giving the bookmark to a friend or loved one who has not experienced the joy of giving thanks to God for His many blessings, especially the forgiveness of sins through faith in Jesus.

Lesson 2   Prayers of the Repentant: The Pharisee and the Tax Collector

Luke 18:9–14

Our Itinerary

In this session we will explore how repentant faith is the vital ingredient in the prayers of the believer. We will focus on the attitude Christians have through faith when approaching their Father in heaven. We will also share with one another the importance of confession and its role in the lives of Christians.

Invited into the Adventure

Amber and her mother were close. The Christian faith they shared drew them even closer. Ever since Amber came home from a semester at the university and started to attend the local junior college, she and her mother had a lot more time together. Amber's Christian boyfriend, Chad, was also happy to have her back. But he and Amber weren't always happy together. One night Amber came home from an uncomfortable date with Chad. Let's listen to her discussion with her mother, Brenda.

Amber: Mom, have you been waiting up for me?

Brenda: No, silly, I was up making out a new prayer list. How's Chad?

Amber: A pain. A big pain.

Brenda: What's wrong, dear?

Amber: Oh, Chad just makes me so angry. We got into a big fight over his lack of faith.

Brenda: What do you mean, sweetie?

Amber: Well, ever since his transmission broke down and the new one cleaned out his savings account, all he does is worry about where he will get enough money to pay his tuition. He doesn't even take me to new-release movies anymore. We just go to the dollar movies. But the worst thing is that he loses his temper every time I ask him to exercise his faith a little more.

Brenda: I know how you feel, dear. Your father was the same way until he began to place more trust in Jesus for his financial needs. But just look at how well God has taken care of things for us. Now we're able to afford any tuition you might need!

Amber: I know! I've been trying to tell Chad how happy we can be when we put Jesus first in our lives.

Brenda: I think this is something we should pray about together. Let's do that right now. . . . Father, we come before You now and thank You for filling us with Your Holy Spirit so that we always make You number one in our lives. Thank You, Jesus, for being real to us and becoming our Lord and our Savior. We thank You for making us truly on fire for You. We ask You now to help Chad to put You first in his life too and rely on You as his Lord. . . .

Meanwhile, while he was driving home, Chad prayed, "Dear God, even though I'm about the worst sinner around and I don't deserve one good thing from You, please forgive me on account of the fact that Jesus died for me. Please give me a fresh start—again."

Let's Talk

1. Amber and Chad were experiencing tension over their differing feelings toward Chad's finances.

a. What appears to be Chad's spiritual need?

b. How does Amber deal with Chad's need?

c. How might she improve or change her approach?

2. How would you characterize Amber and Brenda's ability to pray together? What might a family do to develop a prayer environment like theirs?

3. Take a careful look at Brenda's prayer.
a. For what does she thank God?

b. For what does she ask God?

c. How might Chad have felt if he had heard the prayer?

d. Evaluate Brenda's prayer on the basis of **1 John 1:8–9.**

4. Review the prayer Chad prayed on his way home. In what way might it be a better model of a Christian prayer than Brenda's?

I Should Pray with Confidence! Right?
1. Read **James 1:5–8.**
a. What does this passage make clear about how we are to pray?

b. How might the way we pray change as the things or situations for which we pray change?

2. Read **Luke 18:9–12.**
To whom did Jesus address this parable?

3 a. What words in the Pharisee's prayer show his confidence in his own ability to earn God's favor?

b. How does his confidence in his own abilities make his prayer useless and void?

c. Let's give the Pharisee the benefit of the doubt and suppose that he was "not like other men." Read **Romans 3:23** and **James 2:10.** Even if the Pharisee were grateful to God, what was still wrong with his prayer and his attitude?

d. How can we avoid the trap of spiritual pride as we pray?

4. The Pharisee's prayer shows that he looked down on others, specifically the tax collector. Yet he offered thanks to God.

a. How much would it mean to you if you received thanks from someone who treated one of your loved ones with contempt?

b. How did the Pharisee's attitude toward others make his prayer null and void?

c. In what ways can a life of daily repentance keep us from looking down on others?

5. The Pharisee considered himself superior to the tax collector. How might this explain why he failed to make any requests of God? Read **Mark 1:15.** What two-fold prerequisite was the Pharisee missing? Why is praying pointless without these?

Confident in Christ

1. St. Paul had at one time been a Pharisee. He, like the Pharisee in Jesus' parable, had confidence in his own righteousness. Read Paul's story in **Philippians 3:1–9.** Based on these verses, how do you think St. Paul's prayer life changed as he was motivated by God's love for him in Jesus?

2. In prayer we act out our fellowship with God. God invites us, once enemies, to come to Him as sons and daughters through faith in Jesus. **1 John 1:3** speaks of this fellowship. Read **1 John 1:8–10.** What happens to our fellowship with God if we refuse to confess our sins?

3. Many contemporary, subtle forms of the Pharisee's self-confidence and self-righteousness exist today. Which of the following statements have you heard or are you tempted to say?
"Lord, I've done all I can. You take care of the rest."
"I've been faithful in praying. Lord, You should answer."
"I try hard to be a good person. That should account for some special blessing."

The Confidence to Confess

1. Read **Luke 18:13–14.** If found speaking and behaving this way in a public place, this man would probably be labeled as "suffering from low self-esteem."

a. How did Jesus "classify" him?

b. Upon what did this man depend?

2. Let's be careful not to get the wrong idea here. Was Jesus saying that God would reward this man for his humble attitude and because he did not judge others? No! For all we know, the man might have confessed the fact that he had looked down on others all week! The point is not that this man was good. Instead, he willingly admitted his sin. For what did the tax collector pray? Notice, the tax collector did not pray for the strength and guidance to change his ways. He may have prayed for that later. Instead, at that point, the tax collector sought God's mercy to straighten out the relationship between God and him that had been destroyed by sin.

If a man throws a rock through his neighbor's window, it would not be wise for him to go immediately to his neighbor and ask for a sandwich so he would have the strength to fix the window. Instead, he would go and ask his neighbor for forgiveness. His relationship with his neighbor is most important. So it is between the sinner and God.

3. The tax collector did not merely list some of his sins. He called himself a sinner. Why is it important for us to confess our sinful nature?

4. Given what we have learned today, we might conclude that an unwillingness to confess sin to God is at the root of a meager prayer life. Share, if you like, a time when confession and the declaration of forgiveness through Jesus' sacrificial death was the "breakthrough" you needed in your prayer life.

5. Reread the parable and pay special attention to the posture of the two men. The temple, of course, was a place of public worship. What might this indicate about our posture during the public confession of sin, the clothing we choose to wear for public worship, and the music we use in our public worship.

Venturing Out Together
Read or sing *LW* 232 or *TLH* 317.

Lesson 3   Not As I Will but As You Will: Jesus in Gethsemane

Matthew 26:36–46

Our Itinerary

In this session we will meet Jesus praying in the Garden of Gethsemane as He anguishes over His impending suffering and death. We will observe Jesus as He draws close to His Father in prayer and seeks the consolation and support of His disciples. We will investigate how Jesus' suffering and death on the cross enables us to pray confidently to God at all times. Through faith we can echo Jesus' words, "Yet not as I will, but as You will," confident that His will is always best.

Invited into the Adventure

Ted had known he had something wrong with him. He had avoided going to the doctor because he feared the news. But recently the symptoms had become so bad he decided to visit his doctor. Exploratory surgery revealed that he had cancer throughout much of his body. The doctors told him that the only thing they could do was to keep him comfortable during his last days. Ted's sister Shirley, a dedicated church member and an avid intercessor, had called her church's prayer chain as soon as she found out about her brother's condition. She spoke with Cassandra, the prayer chain leader.

Cassandra: Hello, this is the Ramirez residence.

Shirley: Hi, Cassandra. This is Shirley. How are you?

Cassandra: I'm fine, Shirley, but you sound a little shook. Is everything okay?

Shirley: As long as I trust in the power of prayer, everything will be fine!

Cassandra: What's going on, Shirley?

Shirley: I just got a phone call from Houston—you know, where my brother Ted lives. His wife says he's got cancer and that the doctors say it's too late to do anything for him. So I called you because I know there's plenty we can do for him. We can pray for him.

Cassandra: Oh, Shirley, I'm so sorry. Ted's so young!

Shirley: No need for all that! We're going to lick this thing. You know what prayer can do!

Cassandra: You're right. Our Lord can do great things. What would you like to ask Him?

Shirley: What kind of a crazy question is that? For healing, of course! We're going to claim healing for Ted. Those doctors will be shocked when they discover no trace of cancer anywhere in Ted's body!

Cassandra: Well, that would be great, Shirley. And I'm willing to ask God to heal him . . . according to His own will. But you realize that we can't be sure what God's immediate will is.

Shirley: I've always felt like I could count on you. Jesus said, "Where two or three come together in My name, there am I with them." I was hoping you and I, at least, could make two. But if you can't pray with faith and confidence, I'm sorry but I'll have to look for someone else. I thought you, of all people, believed in the power of prayer.

Cassandra: Shirley, I can see why you're upset right now. But I promise you I'll pray for you and your brother with faith and confidence. But my faith and confidence are in God, not in prayer. When we pray in His name, we leave the outcome up to Him. I'm sure you realize that, don't you Shirley? I don't think we should leave this to a phone conversation. Would you mind if I come over to your place? I feel like you need some support right now. See you in a few minutes?

Shirley: No . . . really . . . I'm fine. I'll get the strength I need from prayer.

Let's Talk

1. As soon as she heard about her brother's condition, Shirley's first impulse was to pray. What are some other ways people react in times of crisis?

2. Shirley seems to feel very confident that with enough of the right kind of prayer, Ted will be healed of his cancer. Naturally, she may be experiencing denial. Does she have any good reason to believe Ted's cancer might be taken away?

3. Cassandra said she was willing to pray for Ted's healing. She also promised she would pray for both Shirley and Ted. What might she include in her prayers?

4. Both Shirley and Cassandra seem to have confidence. In what does each seem to place her confidence?

5. Shirley seems to avoid revealing her emotional needs to her sister in Christ. What might cause this avoidance? What view of God does Shirley reflect in her behavior? in her "faith in prayer"?

Overwhelmed with Sorrow

The prayer life of Jesus Christ, and especially His prayer the night before His death in the Garden of Gethsemane, can serve as a good model for us as we pray. But it is much more than a model! The prayer of our Lord that night, His sufferings, and His victory over Satan that followed, enable us to pray "our Father" to His Father with confidence. Read **Matthew 26:36–46.**

1. Notice **verses 37–38.** What was Jesus' emotional condition as He began to pray? How does each of the following pairs of verses from **Matthew 26** help explain Jesus' emotional condition?

Verses 1 and 2 _____

Verses 7 and 12 _____

Verses 31 and 34 _____

2. We can gain an even fuller understanding of the significance of Jesus' emotions—"overwhelmed with sorrow"—as we read **Isaiah 53:3–7.**

a. How does this prophecy describe Jesus' emotional state as the one who has suffered for us (see **v. 3**)?

b. What did this "suffering servant" do for us according to this prophecy?

c. How does the fact that "the Lord has laid on Him the iniquity of us all" **(v. 6)** open communication between us and our Father in heaven?

May This Cup Be Taken

1. Reread **Matthew 26:39, 42.** This dreaded cup is the cup of God's wrath referred to in other places in Holy Scripture (**Job 21:20; Psalm 75:8; Isaiah 51:17, 22; Revelation 14:10; 16:19**). If Jesus hadn't consumed this cup for us, we would still have to drink it. We would be under the frightful wrath of God. How would that kind of relationship with God affect our freedom to pray to Him?

2. Jesus submitted to His Father's will. For us He drank the cup of His Father's wrath so that we would receive His Father's approval and acceptance.

a. Read **Hebrews 5:7–10.** Of what did Jesus, our High Priest, become the source for us **(v. 9)?**

b. Read **Hebrews 4:14–16.** Why may we approach the throne of grace with confidence?

Into Sinners' Hands

1. Reread **Matthew 26:43–45.** Jesus is painfully aware that the coming of His betrayer means that He will soon be delivered "into the hands of sinners." On several previous occasions, He referred to His coming sufferings and death. Read **Matthew 20:25–28.** What did Jesus accomplish for us and all people by paying a ransom?

2. Read **John 16:17–28.** Once again, Jesus prepares His disciples for His death and resurrection. According to His words here, how does faith in Jesus affect our ability to request things from God the Father? On the basis of this passage, why do Christians pray in Jesus' name?

Prayer and Companionship

Reread **Matthew 26:38, 40.** According to His human nature, Jesus had a strong desire for companionship during His last hours. Notice that even though He is God, He was not too proud or too self-sufficient to seek the companionship of His disciples. What might this suggest to us about our prayers? Read **Hebrews 10:22–25** for help.

In the end, Jesus was left to pray without human companionship. He did not let this keep Him from praying. An absence of human companionship need never keep us from acting on the friendship Jesus established for us with God. God invites us to come to Him in prayer in all places and at all times.

Prayer and Spiritual Warfare

1. Reread **Matthew 26:38–41.** Count the number of times *watch* is used. Jesus urged His disciples to watch and pray. Instead they did the very opposite—they slept. Why is spiritual watchfulness necessary (see **1 Peter 5:8**)?

2. In what ways do you think praying helps us watch? What specific purpose does Jesus have in mind when He instructs His disciples to watch and pray **(verse 41)?** Share, if you like, a time when watchfulness and prayer protected you from falling into temptation.

Prayer and the Will of God

1. Reexamine Jesus' words to His Father.
a. What does Jesus desire?

b. Does Jesus appear to think He will get what He wants? Why might He suspect that He won't get what He wants?

c. Why does He bother to ask?

d. Sometimes we want God to give us something that we think we cannot reasonably expect Him to give us. Why is it important to pray even then?

2. First, Jesus tells His Father what He wants. But then, right away, He tells His Father to do as His Father wills.

a. What might be the purpose in telling God to do what He wills?

b. Share a time when you've prayed, "Not as I will, but as You will."

3. What has Jesus done? (Choose the best answer.)

_____ Jesus assigned His will to His Father's will.

_____ Jesus resigned Himself to His Father's will.

_____ Jesus aligned His will to His Father's will.

4. Prayer is sometimes referred to as "the moving of God's heart." Why might it also be considered the "moving of the heart of the believer"?

5. It was not possible for the human race to have salvation without Jesus' drinking the cup of wrath. At the heart of the Father's will was the Father's love.

a. In what way does this give us good reason to pray, "Not as I will, but as You will"?

b. How can we pray with confidence even when it seems that God's will is different from ours?

Venturing Out Together

1. Read or sing *LW* 422 or *TLH* 521.

2. Review the opening script. Roleplay or discuss possible things Cassandra might say to Shirley concerning God's will as she meets to pray with her.

Lesson 4   Prayers for Special Needs: Peter Released from Prison

Acts 12:1–19

Our Itinerary

In this session we will explore how God sometimes gives us more than we request. We will examine our own prayer history and share times in which God has done more for us than we asked of Him. We will also learn that His greatest gifts—especially the gifts of forgiveness of sins and eternal life through His Son's death—are sometimes things we never would have thought to request.

Invited into the Adventure

Herb and Florence had experienced a rich life together. They had reared five children through tough times, had served in various capacities in their church, and had enjoyed visiting all of their 17 grandchildren and two great-grandchildren. But suddenly the rest of their life together didn't look very bright. Doctors had diagnosed Herb with terminal cancer. Let's listen as Herb speaks with his pastor in the hospital room.

Pastor: Herb, you know that our Lord has been very good to you over the years. He's taken good care of you. He's going to do that now too. Just as the psalmist says, "God is our refuge and strength, an ever-present help in trouble" **(Ps. 46:1).**

Herb: Thank you, Pastor, I need that reminder. I've always hoped it would be my heart that would take me—quickly. This disease is what I have always feared the most. The pain scares me. Pastor, I'm afraid. I'm afraid of losing my faith because of this.

Pastor: Herb, you remember those familiar words of David in **Psalm 23,** "Yea, though I walk through the valley of the shadow of death, I will fear no evil: for Thou art with me; Thy rod and thy staff they comfort me" (KJV). We pass through the valley of the shadow of death, but we don't remain stuck in it. And as we go through, our Shepherd goes with us. And with the rod and staff of His Word He fights off the enemies that try to attack us. Those enemies are guilt, fear that God doesn't love us, and bitterness toward God for allowing us to suffer. Your Good Shepherd will help you fight off those enemies. Let's ask Him for that help right now. Okay?

Herb: Sounds like a good idea to me.

Pastor: Heavenly Father, You have promised to be our refuge and strength. You have promised to be our ever-present help in time of trouble. And You have promised to be with us and protect us as we walk through the valley of the shadow of death. For these great and firm promises we thank You. For the assurance of complete forgiveness on account of Christ we thank You. We ask You, Father, to make Your presence known to Your son and servant, Herb. Comfort and strengthen him in the days of trial ahead. O Lord, enable Herb to fight this last battle and win the victory that's already his in Christ. Protect him from the assaults of the evil one. And grant him, we pray, both a peaceful death and a joyful awakening in heaven. Amen.

Herb: Thank you, Pastor. I feel stronger already.

(A few days later the phone in Pastor Wilson's study rang. It was Herb.)

Herb: Pastor, you're never going to believe this. They ran some more tests on me. Pastor, the tumors are gone! Gone! The doctors say that happens sometimes. We know who makes it happen, don't we, Pastor?

Let's Talk

1. What fears did Herb express to his pastor? Why do you think Herb expressed concern about his faith? How might you have felt in Herb's situation?

2. What spiritual enemies did Herb's pastor identify? In what ways did he help Herb begin to battle those enemies? For what sorts of things did Herb's pastor pray? For what did he *not* pray? Share, if you like, things for which you forget to pray.

3. If you were Herb's pastor, what sorts of feelings might you have had when you found out Herb's tumors were gone? Do you think this experience would change the way you pray on such occasions? Was there anything *wrong* with the way Herb's pastor prayed?

A Special Need for Prayer

At some times, more than at others, it is very easy for us to see that we need to pray. There were also such times in the life of the earliest Christians. Read **Acts 12:1–5.** By this time Stephen had been stoned to death **(Acts 7).** Saul and other leaders in Jerusalem had been persecuting the church. Herod "had James, the brother of John, put to death with the sword" (most likely beheaded). The Herod mentioned in our text was Agrippa I, the grandson of Herod the Great who tried to kill the infant Jesus **(Matthew 2).** He was also a nephew to Herod Antipas who killed John the Baptist **(Mark 6:14–29)** and ridiculed Jesus before His crucifixion **(Luke 23:11).**

1. According to **Acts 12:3,** why did Herod arrest Peter?

2 a. According to **verses 3–4,** at what time of the year did Peter's arrest take place? Consider the time of Jesus' death **(Luke 22:15).** What was the significance of this timing?

b. Certainly the other believers in Jerusalem were conscious of this connection. Given Jesus' teaching about the persecution of His followers **(John 15:20),** what might the believers in Jerusalem have concluded about Peter's imprisonment? Assuming they were aware of the events recorded in **John 21:17–19,** what might they have feared would happen to Peter?

3. Verse 12 makes it clear that some of the disciples had gathered for prayer. What risks did they take by doing this? Why do you think they were inclined to take such risks?

4. What might be some special reasons for believers today to gather for prayer? Share an occasion in which you gathered with believers to pray. What current events in the life of your congregation or community might prompt people to gather to pray?

A Special Prayer for Special Needs

We know the church prayed for Peter **(Acts 12:5),** but we do not know for what the believers prayed. The book of Acts records some of the prayers of the early believers. The epistles of St. Paul also give us a glimpse into the prayer life of the early church.

1 a. Read **Acts 4:23–31.** The believers viewed Peter and John's imprisonment in the light of the Old Testament Scriptures **(vv. 25–26)** and the life and death of Jesus **(vv. 27–28).** How could this help them respond to suffering (see **Matthew 5:1–12** and **1 Peter 4:13**)?

b. How did their view of suffering affect their prayer? For what did they pray?

c. Despite the threats of the Jewish leaders, what prayer request is *not* mentioned in the text? How can this prayer be a model for us?

d. Later, in our text, when Peter was imprisoned again, how might the disciples' prayers have been similar? different?

2 a. Read **Ephesians 6:19–20** and **Colossians 4:3–4.** For what does St. Paul ask the believers to pray concerning him and his ministry?

b. Is your pastor's ministry more often the subject of conversation or the subject of prayer? How might these prayer requests of St. Paul benefit your pastor and church leaders and their ministry?

c. Do you think prayers of this sort might have been prayed on Peter's behalf during his imprisonment? Why or why not?

3 a. Read **Romans 15:31** and **2 Thessalonians 3:2.** For what does St. Paul ask believers to pray in these verses?

b. Does it seem likely that such prayers were offered in Peter's behalf on the night of the events recorded in our text? Why or why not?

c. Can you think of some Christians for which we might pray similar prayers today?

A Special God Who Gives beyond Our Need

1. Read **Acts 12:6–19.** What did Peter think until the time the angel left him **(v. 9)?** What might this suggest about the content of his prayers concerning his imprisonment? Peter was sleeping. What does this show about his confidence in his God?

2. Peter got out of prison and got away from guards but at first he couldn't get into Mark's mother's house. When Rhoda announced Peter's presence, what did the others think she had seen **(v. 15)?** What does this suggest about their expectations? their prayers?

3. As the early Christians knew so well, our Lord has invited His followers into a life that often includes the privilege and glory of suffering. Since Jesus Christ destroyed the works of the devil **(1 John 3:8)** by means of suffering **(Hebrews 2:14),** believers are motivated to do the same by remaining stubbornly faithful to Him amidst various kinds of suffering. During such times, it is good and right to pray for things like boldness, courage, faithfulness, and strength. And sometimes God answers that prayer by saying, "I'll do that and more." At those times He delivers us from our current suffering and continues to strengthen our faith through His Word and Sacrament to enable us to triumph amidst future suffering. In this way God gives us more than we ask or could imagine. Sometimes we may not be able to imagine that God could mightily deliver us from our present sufferings. What a delightful surprise when He does!

4. Consider this fact: St. Peter was most likely prepared for martyrdom. Do you think it may have taken him a while to adjust to the fact that this honor would not yet be his? Peter didn't turn around, leave the angel, and head for the prison entrance shouting, "Take me! I want to suffer for my Lord!" What does this say to us when we are prepared to suffer for God?

5. There have been thousands of Christian prisoners and martyrs over the centuries. Often God has not spared them from their confinement and suffering but rather has enabled them to triumph within it. According to church history, St. Peter himself was eventually martyred. Peter's experience in **Acts 12** is the exception rather than the rule. Yet what does this exception teach us about the God to whom we pray? In heaven Peter's experience will be the rule. No exceptions!

6. Although Peter's experience is an exception, God's over-abundant generosity is the rule! If you'd like to do so, share with one another times in which you or someone you know has received from God more than asked of Him. In what way is Jesus' death and resurrection for us (and the life that's ours as a result) something more than we could ask or imagine?

Venturing Out Together
 Read or sing *LW* 286 or *TLH* 351.

Lesson 5   Praising God: Miriam's Song of Praise

Exodus 15:1–21

Our Itinerary

In this session we explore prayers of praise to God. We praise God for who He is and for what He has done for us as Creator, Redeemer, and Sanctifier. This session will also put us in touch with some songs of praise used by fellow believers over the centuries. The expressions of praise we share with them can enhance and enrich both our public and our private worship.

Invited into the Adventure

As he tightened his life jacket and stepped off the dock into the commercial touring boat, Willis Kohl was delighted to see how clear and bright the water was at Rainbow Haven. He was even happier to see the smiling eyes of his hosts. He commented, "Now this is one of those perks nobody mentioned when I was in law school."

Each year hosts of tourists paid dearly for this trip, but today Willis rode as a guest. His hosts—a group of local merchants, fishermen, and nature lovers—made it clear to him that they felt he deserved this tour. Let's listen in.

Karl: I'll never generalize about lawyers again! I'll tell you what, Mr. Kohl, you've destroyed one of my stereotypes about lawyers!

Wally: Mr. Kohl isn't just any lawyer, Karl. He's a government attorney. He works for the people. He's there to help us!

Stan: That's for sure. We'd be in a real mess if it weren't for you, Willis. On our own there's no way we could have stopped Omnilube from dumping their chemical waste into this river. But you sure stopped them!

Karl: You sunk those guys in the ooze of their own fake data!

Kent: And, thanks to your stubborn efforts, they've even had to clean up the mess they made around here!

Wally: Next time somebody tries messing with this river, we'll know where to turn. With your help we'll plug up their sludge spouts before they can open the valves! They put their toughest attorneys on this case and you sent them home crying to Mommy!

Karl: It really is good to know we don't have to stand by and put up with this sort of thing.

Kent: That's right. You know, Mr. Kohl, you're getting a reputation around here. You really blasted them! I think those Omnilube guys start sweating when they get a glimpse of your agency's letterhead!

Karl: And now they're a bit more cautious around us too!

Wally: You know what? It seems like this is more than a job for you, Willis. I get the feeling you do this kind of thing because you care.

Stan: Come on, you guys. I think you're embarrassing Mr. Kohl.

Karl: Well he deserves to hear this. And it just seems right to finally say it straight to his face. I can't help showing him my appreciation.

Let's Talk

1. How might life have looked for the people of Rainbow Haven if Willis had not battled for them? What dangers would we face if it weren't for our advocate, Jesus Christ? (See **1 John 2:1.**)

2. How did Willis seem to feel when he saw the new condition of the river and his hosts' eyes? Read **Hebrews 12:2.** What was the "joy set before" Jesus?

3. What sort of relationship did Willis seem to have with Omnilube's attorneys? Why was this relationship apparently necessary? Read **1 John 3:8** and **Hebrews 2:14–15.** In what ways might Jesus' ministry be described as fierce and destructive?

4. Speaking well of Willis and celebrating as a community had become the same thing. Why is this so? About what and about whom do Christians wish to speak when they gather in the presence of their Advocate and Deliverer?

5. Willis' hosts told and retold the good news of his past acts done for them. How did the telling and retelling affect their view of their future? Can the same be said about worship in your congregation? in your personal and/or family devotional life?

Great Conquest: No Wonder There's Praising Going On!

As invigorating and exciting as it is to see a river cleaned up, we Christians have a much greater reason for robust celebration. Throughout history those who know the living God and His activity on their behalf have celebrated in worship. Read **Exodus 15:1–21** and discuss the following:

1. Skim the chapters prior to this chapter. Summarize the events that occurred just prior to those of our text. From what did God save the Israelites? How does this help explain why the people eagerly praise God?

2 a. What language of warfare is used in these verses?

b. In what ways is the Egyptian defeat described?

c. How are Pharaoh and his soldiers depicted in **verse 9?**

d. Take a closer look at how Egypt is treated. It seems as if Israel is boasting. What does the contrast between Egypt's pride and apparent strength and its ultimate frailty and shame actually help to underscore? In what way does Israel's slave status help underscore this even more fully?

e. Read **1 Corinthians 1:26–31** and **Galatians 6:14.** In what do Christians boast?

3 a. In identifying and talking about their enemy the people of Israel were able to identify the enormity of the victory God had provided. Read **1 Corinthians 15:21–26.** What is our enemy in these verses? How has Jesus Christ already begun defeating death?

b. Read **2 Thessalonians 2:7–10.** According to these verses, what other enemy will Christ destroy upon His return?

c. Read **Romans 5:7–11.** Based on these verses, list the big victories with which we credit our Deliverer, Jesus Christ.

Great Content: Don't Try to Praise without It!

The Israelites were obviously very excited after crossing the sea on dry ground and watching the Egyptians drown amidst their hot pursuit. God's children were clearly full of emotion. But that emotion didn't keep their praise from being full of content. They gave God specific titles (strength, song, salvation, warrior, etc.). They spoke both of specific deeds God had done and of specific qualities God possesses (**verse 11,** for example). Their praise involved both their heads and their hearts. Choose one of the following songs of praise in use in the New Testament church. What titles does it give God? What does it say about God's deeds? about God's qualities?

1. The Gloria in Excelsis (*LW* pp. 138–39, *TLH* pp. 17–19)

2. This is the feast (*LW* pp. 161–63)

3. The Venite (*LW* pp. 209–11, *TLH* pp. 33–34)

4. The Te Deum Laudamus (*LW* pp. 214–17 or #8, *TLH* pp. 35–37)

Great Confidence: Let's Look Ahead with Our Praising!

Reread **Exodus 15:13–18** and discuss the following:

1. How did the Israelites' recent experience affect their view of their future? The various nations and peoples mentioned here were those with whom the Israelites would have to battle in order to take possession of the land promised by God. What was their attitude about these upcoming battles? Upon what was this attitude based? How can our praise of God prepare us for our future?

2. Take a few minutes to discuss parts of the future about which many people often feel fear or anxiety. Now think back over this session and some of the Scripture passages and the songs of praise you've read and discussed. How can God's qualities and deeds help us face these fears and anxieties about the future?

3. Christian worship looks ahead to the ultimate victory and bliss that Christ earned for us by His death and resurrection but that won't be completely visible to us until our Lord returns from heaven or until we're called to be with Him in heaven. In the Lord's Prayer we rejoice that our Father owns "the kingdom and the power and the glory forever." In the Nicene Creed we express our firm expectation, "and He will come again with glory. . . . I look for the resurrection of the dead and the life of the world to come." In the Te Deum we ask confidently to be "numbered with your saints in glory everlasting." We sing of a "foretaste of the feast to come" (*LW* p. 169). How can our sure and happy future help us deal with the struggles of our present experience? If you like, share a time when your anticipation of heaven enabled you to face times of trouble with confidence.

4. Read **Exodus 15:22–24.** The Israelites changed as they began to face tough times. We often do the same. How can we continue to praise our God even when we face difficult times?

Venturing Out Together

1. Pray together one or more of the songs of praise studied in this lesson.

2. Create a song of praise that focuses on the attributes of God and His activity in your life. Share your song of praise with a partner or the entire group.

3. Read or sing *LW* 126.

Lesson 6   Our Privilege in Prayer: Elijah and the Prophets of Baal

1 Kings 18:16–40

Our Itinerary

In this session we will examine some false notions people have about prayer. As we study God's Word, we will have the opportunity to gain a deeper understanding of the privilege God gives us in prayer as a result of the relationship He established between us and Him through Jesus.

Invited into the Adventure

Lance and Tricia were on their way home from church. They both had strong reactions to the sermon they had just heard. Let's listen in as they discuss it.

Lance: Boy, that was one of Pastor Zellmer's best sermons yet. Don't you think?

Tricia: Hardly! I'm sorry, Lance, but I think sometimes Pastor Zellmer is so heavenly minded he's no earthly good. All this business about praying for our daily bread. I'll bet lots of people have starved doing that. Tangible problems and issues need tangible solutions.

Lance: Say, somehow that reminds me. Didn't you say we needed to stop at Pause & Pay on the way home?

Tricia: We sure do. We need to pick up some milk and some chips. Oh, and we need to pick up a couple more lottery tickets. My horoscope says this is a good time for me to do some investing. We need to do something to boost our income.

Lance: So, back to the sermon. I thought it was just what we've been needing lately.

Tricia: Well, I'm glad you enjoyed it. I can think of about six other things I would have rather listened to.

Lance: So you don't think it would help if we relied more on God for our daily bread?

Tricia: Maybe we can count on Him for bread. But what I'm worried about is the cost of butter and clothes and rent and all our credit card bills. God hasn't exactly taken care of those things!

Lance: Oh, I'm sorry. I just passed Pause & Pay.

Tricia: That's okay. We haven't reached the limit on our credit card. Let's eat out again tonight. We work hard for our money. We deserve it. I feel like some pizza. How about you?

Lance: Sure. Pizza would be fine. Maybe going out to eat will cheer you up a little.

Tricia: You're right. Our finances have depressed me lately. Of course, I haven't imaged our wealth enough lately either. That's probably the main problem! Do you know where I stuck my Rich Imagination tapes?

Lance: You mean those tapes that teach you to meditate wealth into existence by tuning into cosmic energy?

Tricia: Those are the ones.

Lance: I think they're either in the ski boat or in the motor home.

Tricia: Man! Three weekends in a row at the lake and I haven't even had a chance to meditate! No wonder we have problems.

Let's Talk

1. What was apparently bothering Tricia? How might Pastor Zellmer's sermon have helped Tricia if she wouldn't have rejected it? What do you think of her statement about tangible problems needing tangible solutions? Do you think God gives tangible solutions to those who pray to Him in faith?

2. Tricia felt God wasn't coming through for her when it came to her financial needs. How might you explain the apparent financial problems she and Lance were having? To what did Tricia attribute the money she and Lance had? Does she think of God as her provider? How might this affect her spending? her prayer life? her attitude about her financial condition? her attitude concerning the sermon?

3. On what did Tricia depend to improve her and Lance's financial picture? How did her reliance on these things affect her ability to rely on God? Why might these things have seemed more reliable than God?

4. If you were a close friend of Tricia or Lance, what might you say to help?

5. What might cause a Christian to feel that it won't do any good to pray for help with temporal things?

Praying Around

Perhaps you've seen a dog chase its own tail. Now just imagine a talking dog chasing its tail for hours and yelping to its master, "Help! I'm feeling dizzy. Please! Make me not feel dizzy!" That's about how silly we look when we ask God to help us, and yet we continue to focus on the things that hurt us.

The people of ancient Israel once lived that way. Their king, Ahab, married a pagan woman, Jezebel. King Ahab started worshiping her false god, Baal (1 Kings 16:29–33). Other Israelites worshiped Baal too. They thought Baal might make their crops grow better. They also kept worshiping and praying to the true God. They tried to cover all the bases.

But God wanted His people to know that He is the only one who rules and sustains nature. So God sent a drought to show that worshiping nature-gods doesn't work. Queen Jezebel missed the point and started threatening and killing God's spokesmen, the prophets. She probably thought Baal stopped the rain because she tolerated God's prophets and the message they shared. For this reason the prophet Elijah hid in exile. But one day God decided He and Elijah would get aggressive. Read **1 Kings 18:16–40.** Then discuss the following questions.

1. What had to happen before God would send rain to Israel (see **verses 36–37**)?

2 a. According to **verses 16–18,** upon whom did Ahab blame Israel's troubles?

b. Whose fault were they really?

c. Baal worshipers believed Baal controlled nature and affected the size of the harvest. Why do you think God stopped the rain in Israel?

3 a. Reread **verse 21.** Describe Israel's spiritual condition.

b. Read **James 1:5–8.** Can double-mindedness exist with faith? How does double-mindedness impact the effectiveness of a person's prayer? Can you think of some examples of double-mindedness today?

.

4 a. Now read **James 4:6–10** and **5:16–18.** What solution does God's Word provide for double-mindedness?

b. How does a person become righteous? (See **Romans 3:21–24.**) Why do you think the prayers of a righteous person are effective?

Prayer Necessities

When we examine Elijah's prayer, we can see that "effective" prayers are quite simple when compared to the prayers of those who tragically and futilely cling to false gods. Let's compare the praying of the prophets of Baal with Elijah's prayer:

Pray Longer?

Reread **1 Kings 18:26–29.**

1. For how long did the prophets of Baal pray? Time Elijah's prayer in **verses 36–37.** How does the amount of time in prayer affect the outcome?

2. Read **Matthew 6:7–13.** Why don't we need to repeat ourselves over and over when praying to our Father in heaven?

3. On the other hand, what good reasons might a believer have for spending a large amount of time in prayer?

Pray Stronger?
Review **1 Kings 18:26–29.**
1. Describe the actions of the prophets of Baal as they prayed. How did they hope to get Baal's attention? Why is such self-abuse unnecessary for the Christian at prayer?

2. Reread Elijah's prayer in **verses 36–37.** What did Elijah do to get God's attention?

3. Christians don't need to shed their own blood in order to get God to listen to their prayers. Why not? (See **Hebrews 9:14–15.**)

Strength in Numbers?
How many prophets of Baal prayed? Just one prophet of God prayed. That was enough. Yet our Lord does encourage us to pray with one or two others. He doesn't do so in order to make our prayer "worth God's while." One person praying in faith has God's attention. When might a Christian have to stand alone in prayer?

Purposeful Prayer
1. Once again examine Elijah's prayer in **verses 36–37.** Surprisingly, for what did Elijah *not* ask? For what did he ask?

2. Elijah prayed that the Israelites would know that God was in control. But Elijah also prayed that they would know that he himself was God's prophet sent by God. Why was this important to Israel's spiritual health? Why is recognizing God's ordained spokesmen still important to the spiritual health of believers today? (See **Luke 10:16.**)

Putting It All Together

Use what you have learned in this session to complete the following statements.

1. My prayers *do not* _____

_____

because _____

2. My prayers are acceptable to God because _____

_____

3. Is it possible to pray without faith? Why or why not?

Venturing Out Together

1. Read or sing *LW* 299 or *TLH* 447.

2. Consider the script at the beginning of this session. What might you say to Lance and Tricia? If time permits, roleplay possible outcomes.

3. What would you say to each of the following people?

- "If I would have just prayed harder, maybe God would have answered."
- "I don't need to pray because God already knows what I'm thinking."
- "Depend on God? Not me. I depend on number 1, me!"

Lesson 7 Pray for Victory against Our Enemies: Elisha's Angel Army

2 Kings 6:8–23

Our Itinerary

In this session we see the relationship between prayer and faith. Faith in Jesus encourages and empowers us to pray boldly and confidently for victory against our spiritual enemies—the sinful world, our sinful self, and Satan. It also helps us to respond to the sometimes difficult challenges presented to us by those who don't know Christ as their Savior.

Invited into the Adventure

Genevieve and her young adult niece April are very close. In fact they often spend a good portion of each Sunday afternoon together. This particular afternoon, as usual, they enjoy lunch together after attending church. Let's listen in.

Genevieve: Say, April, this morning in church I noticed that guy you dated a few times several months ago. He's come to church regularly for about three months, hasn't he?

April: Yes. We broke up about four months ago and about a month after that he started showing up at church. There's not much I can do about it.

Genevieve: You don't sound too happy about his church attendance.

April: Well, of course not! I think he's just coming in order to irritate me. You don't understand, but I guess that's not your fault. I never told you why I broke it off with Justin. You see, he got to where he was really applying the pressure, big time, to get me to, you know, do it with him.

Genevieve: So you broke it off! Good for you! You deserve better than that. You deserve a man who takes good care of you.

April: I wish I believed that. I'm afraid I may have made the mistake of my life. What if no one else ever comes along for me? I don't know why God didn't make me pretty like Rachel. Do you know what it's like to have an older sister who's better looking and slimmer than you are?

Genevieve: To tell you the truth, I do. Your mother was always the popular one when we were growing up. Look, you did the right thing. You stood where God's Word stands. What could be wrong with that?

April: I know I did the right thing and all. It's just that sometimes I wonder whether God really loves me. It seems like He gives the really good stuff to other people. I always hoped for advances from a man, but I wanted them to take the form of a candlelight marriage proposal.

Genevieve: Oh, how I wish you could see just how much God does love you. I'll pray for you so you will see that. He wants you to see that.

April: I just wish Justin would blow away. It's bad enough that I have to see him at work, but at church too? I hate small town life! You can't get away from certain people!

Genevieve: Don't you see, April? The devil set a trap for you when he sent Justin along. He thought Justin could snag you for himself. But instead God used you, the Word of God that you shared, and the faith you demonstrated to snag Justin for Himself.

April: Oh, I know I should feel good about it. But sometimes it's so hard to know what to do. Like with Rachel's wedding shower, should we invite Justin's mom or not? She and I got pretty close, but what kind of a signal would that send to Justin?

Genevieve: A signal that the forgiveness he's heard about in church is real.

Let's Talk

1. What seems to bother April the most? What would help her the most?

2. What do you think of Genevieve's plan to pray that God would help April see how much He loves her? If you were Genevieve, what words might your prayer include?

3. What is your reaction to Genevieve's statement, "The devil set a trap for you when he sent Justin along"? What is your reaction to this statement: "God used you . . . to snag Justin"? How does this show God's power over Satan?

4. Based on what you know of the situation, do you think it would be good and wise for April to invite Justin's mother to Rachel's wedding shower? Why or why not? What do you think of Genevieve's response to that question?

An Army of Angels in Every Direction

Read **2 Kings 6:8–17** and discuss the following:

1. What did Elisha do to anger the king of the Arameans?

2. Read **Ephesians 5:11.** What does the Christian do to anger Satan? Can you think of some examples of Christians doing this?

3 a. After Elisha realized the Arameans had surrounded the place where he stayed, what did he pray? What was the result?

b. How is Elisha's prayer similar to or different than a prayer you might pray if you discovered you were surrounded by an enemy?

c. Read **1 Peter 5:8.** Considering this enemy, what might you pray?

The Love of God in Every Direction

1. Read **Ephesians 3:16–19.**

a. What spiritual blessing does Paul ask God to grant to the believers at Ephesus?

b. In what ways is God's love like the angels Elisha's servant couldn't see at first?

c. What sometimes makes it difficult for us to see the full extent of God's love for us?

2 a. Share, if you like, a time when you realized the greatness of God's love for us in Christ. What enables us to know God's love for us in Christ (see **Ephesians 1:13–14**)?

b. Read **Ephesians 2:4–9.** To whom do we credit God's great love for us?

3. Read **Ephesians 1:17–23.** For what does Paul pray that God would grant to the people of Ephesus? How is the Holy Spirit involved in the accomplishing of this? the church?

4. Read **John 14:26.** What does the Holy Spirit do for us? How will this help us see the extent of God's love for us in Christ? How would you describe the availability of the Holy Spirit and His power (see **Luke 11:11–13**)? Check one and then explain.

_____ very available to me

_____ somewhat available to me

_____ not readily available to me

Our Side Is Stronger Than Theirs

1. Reread **2 Kings 6:16.** Elisha could see that he and God had the Arameans outnumbered. How do you think this knowledge affected his perspective?

2. Now read **1 John 4:1–4.** What is it we Christians need to "see" (keep in view) as we do battle with evil spirits, temptation, and the accusations of the devil?

Blindness Traps Israel's Enemy
Read **2 Kings 6:18–20.**
1. Why do you think the Arameans followed Elisha's direction?

2. Samaria was the capital city of Israel, the Northern Kingdom. Why do you suppose Elisha chose that location? How do you imagine the Arameans felt when they realized their location?

Blindness Traps God's Enemies
Read **2 Peter 2:1–10.** What is the destiny of all who remain blinded by sin?

Israel's Kindness Turns an Enemy Around
Read **2 Kings 6:21–23.**
1. This was a fabulous military opportunity for Israel. What would have been the obvious way to put an end to the Arameans' aggressions? What did Elisha do rather than destroy the Arameans?

2. How did Israel's kindness affect the Arameans?

God's Kindness Turns Enemies Around
1 a. Read **Romans 2:4.** What does God's kindness toward us accomplish in us? Can you share an example of this dynamic at work in your life?

b. Read **1 John 4:11.** How is the same dynamic at work in this passage?

2. Read **Romans 12:20–21.** How does God desire the Christian to respond to evil? How might this love mirror the love described in **Romans 5:8?**

Venturing Out Together
1. Read or sing *LW* 362 or *TLH* 371.
2. List some things for which you plan to pray concerning the following:
a. Someone who needs to know better that God loves him or her.
b. An opportunity to overcome evil with good.

Lesson 8 Following God's Will: Solomon's Prayer for Wisdom

2 Chronicles 1:1–12

Our Itinerary
In this session we will explore how to pray in stereo with God's Word and will. As we examine a biblical prayer that was clearly pleasing to God, we will see more clearly what God would like us to include in our prayers. We will also explore how prayer provides an opportunity to cling to God's promises and ask Him to do for us what He has already said He will do.

Invited into the Adventure
Judy and Ramona were good neighbors and fairly close friends. Every Thursday evening they, along with some other ladies from the area, gathered at Ramona's house for Bible study, prayer, and Christian conversation. On this particular evening Judy stayed around after the other women left. She wanted to discuss the ladies' reaction to the prayer request she had made earlier that evening.

Judy: I don't get it. Usually everyone in our group is so warm and supportive. But tonight, judging from the way they all looked at me, you'd think I asked them all to fall on their faces and worship the devil!

Ramona: Maybe I can help you understand . . . (*interrupted*)

Judy: Maybe you can help *them* understand! They need to understand what my son has gone through during the past few years. You should see some of the girls he has brought home: high school dropouts, drug addicts, girls with mental problems. You name it, he's dated it. Now he's met a nice, attractive, born-again, educated girl from a good family and asks her to move in with him. Those women treated me like an outcast just because I ask them to pray that she accepts his invitation!

Ramona: Judy, have you ever heard of "praying the Bible"?

Judy: No, I've heard of reading it and teaching it, but what's this about praying it?

Ramona: "Praying the Bible" means we pray for the things the Bible says God wants to see happen. Someone once said that scientists who study how nature works are just thinking God's thoughts after Him. When we pray this way, it's like we're just willing God's will after Him.

Judy: Well that's no excuse for being rude! I thought we were all equal in this group.

Ramona: Well, Judy, we are. All except One of us. And that One is much wiser than the rest of us. That One is Jesus. He's Lord! We don't want to ever ask Him to make something happen that we know He doesn't *want* to happen. That would be like asking a good doctor for poison!

Judy: Why wouldn't Jesus want my son to be happy?

Ramona: O Judy, He does want your son to be happy. And *He* knows what is best for your son. The ladies here tonight just want to trust God to know what's best for your son. Do you think you can do that too?

Judy: That usually seems to easy. But this time . . .

Ramona: I know. You really want your son to settle down with a good, Christian girl.

Judy: . . . but not to live together before they're married.

Ramona: Then we'll all pray with you! We won't be asking God to do something that disagrees with His will.

Let's Talk

1. Why did Judy feel the other women in the group had been rude to her? How can differences in thinking affect people's ability to pray together?

2. How did Judy and Ramona seem to differ when it came to knowing God's will? On what did Judy tend to base her perceptions of God's will? Ramona?

3. How do you feel about Ramona's description of "praying the Bible"? Share, if you wish, times in which you feel this is how you have prayed. In order to do this "at the drop of a hat," what would a believer have to be doing regularly?

4. At times we want to pray for things about which God gives no clear directions in the Bible. On these occasions should we avoid prayer so we do not pray in disagreement with God's will, ask God to give us what we'd like to have, or what?

5. Match the following situations to the corresponding Scripture-based prayer:

a. A relative is in unbelief.

b. The cashier erred $10.00 in your favor.

c. You're upset you can't afford nicer things.

d. A Christian uncle has cancer.

e. Enemies are slandering your good name.

___ Lord, keep him confident of Your love.

___ "Thy kingdom come."

___ "Lead us not into temptation."

___ Grant them repentance.

___ I have food and clothing. Help me be content with that.

Worship: A Great Prelude to Great Prayer

Worship Is Not Just Alone

1. Read **2 Chronicles 1:1–2.** Solomon brought together a great assembly of leaders in Israel and called them to worship and to inquire of the Lord. Instead, he could have introduced a five-point vision for the nation. What does this early step in Solomon's reign say about his administrative priorities? What does it say about his sense of connectedness with others in Israel?

2. The fall into sin brought about alienation and discord between people. Why is it appropriate that worship of God by those who have been restored to Him should be a communal event? What does this suggest for those who believe they can pray and read their Bible at home?

Worship Is Not Just at Home

1. Read **2 Chronicles 1:3.** A person may feel that as long as two or three gather (**Matthew 18:20**), worship can be done at home just as well as at church. Think about the tabernacle built by Moses. What made it a good place to gather for worship? For help you may wish to scan **Exodus 28–31.**

2. Jesus taught that "the Sabbath was made for man, not man for the Sabbath" (**Mark 2:27**). In what ways has your experience in formal worship helped you develop a sense of God's power and love?

Worship Is Not Just Contemporary

Read **2 Chronicles 1:4–6.** Solomon was to build the temple. He seems to have modeled himself after Bezalel, the expert craftsman who was so useful in the building of the tabernacle during Moses' day. Like Solomon, Bezalel was specifically named and chosen to perform his duties in the building of the place of worship.

Even though the ark of God was right there in Jerusalem, Solomon chose to travel north to Gibeon in order to worship at the altar built 400 years earlier by Bezalel. The setting suggests very formal worship. In what way do your place of worship and your worship practices help reinforce your connection with Christians from centuries past? How does their model help shape your prayers?

A Prayer Model

Read **2 Chronicles 1:7–12** and discuss the following:

A Great Offer

1. Notice **verse 7.** God offered to give Solomon whatever He requested. Of course, God knew in advance what Solomon would request. God wanted to do what Solomon wanted because Solomon wanted what God wanted. If Solomon's character had been such that he would have requested something harmful to himself or others, do you think God would have made this great offer?

2. Read **John 15:7.** These words make it clear that we are to remain in Christ, with His Word remaining in us. How is this condition related to Jesus promising to give us whatever we request?

A Great Prayer Outline

1. Read Solomon's prayer in **2 Chronicles 1:8–10.** How might Solomon's prayer outline (below) be useful for us today as we seek to structure God-pleasing prayers?

a. I praise God for His kindness **(verse 8).**

b. I credit God (or hold Him responsible) for bringing me to this point in my life **(verse 8).**

c. I remind God of His promises and ask Him to keep them **(verse 9).**

d. I ask God to enable me to do the tasks He has given me **(verse 10).**

e. I tell God why I think I need what I've just said I need, once again reminding Him and myself that He gave me this responsibility **(verse 10).**

2. Using this outline, how might Solomon's prayer have looked if he were a mother or father? a pastor? a teacher? you?

3. Read **James 1:5.** Share, if you like, a time when wisdom was just what you needed!

A Greater Wisdom—A Greater Temple

Read **Matthew 12:6, 42** and discuss the following:

Knowing One Greater Than the Temple

The New Testament shows that Jesus is the wisdom of God (**1 Corinthians 1:24, 30** and **Colossians 2:2–3**) and that His body is the temple of God (**John 2:18–22**). What does this mean for those who seek wisdom apart from Jesus? for those who seek a relationship with "the divine" apart from Jesus?

Living as His Body, the Temple

The holy Christian church is the living body of Christ (**1 Corinthians 12:27**), God's temple (**1 Corinthians 3:16; Ephesians 2:21**). Read **James 3:13–17** and describe our life together with other Christians. How is it similar to life in your congregation? How is it related to your new life as redeemed children of God?

Our Praise of Wisdom in the Eternal Temple

1. It all will come together clearly in heaven. Wisdom is one of the characteristics of Christ for which we will praise Him in eternity (**Revelation 5:12** and **7:12**). He and His Father will be our temple there (**Revelation 21:22**). How does this vision of the temple of God in heaven improve your perspective on that temple, Christ's body, here on earth in the church?

2. When Solomon finished building and dedicating the Old Testament temple, he offered a prayer that included these words, "Hear the supplication of your servant and of your people Israel when they pray toward this place. Hear from heaven, your dwelling place, and when you hear, forgive" (**1 Kings 8:30**). Solomon pictured believers praying "toward" the temple. Think of your church building as both that ancient temple and also the heavenly temple converged into the now. How might this picture of your church inspire you as you, each day at home, pray "toward" your church—remembering the faith and the people of your church?

Venturing Out Together

1. Read or sing *LW* 444 or *TLH* 39.

2. Talk to a family member or friend about prayer. What practices (if any) in this person's life help him or her to remember to pray for things he or she knows are things God wants us to have?

3. What are some ways we can strengthen the bond of "praying together" when we are alone?

Lesson 9 Persistence in Prayer: The Parable of a Widow's Prayer

Luke 18:1–8

Our Itinerary

In this session we will explore how to respond when it seems clear that we are praying in agreement with God's expressed will but God seems to ignore our prayer. We will have occasion to see more fully the value of persistence in prayer.

Invited into the Adventure

Nicole had been an active member of St. John's since childhood. But several months ago she suddenly stopped attending worship services. Both her pastor and her elders had repeatedly tried to sit down with her, but she kept refusing. Finally one night, Diane, who had worked closely with Nicole in the singles ministry at St. John's, dropped by Nicole's apartment and sat down with her. It wasn't long before Nicole was sobbing as she struggled to explain her absence from worship services.

Nicole: It's so hard for me to talk about this. It makes me feel filthy every time I think about it. The memories still hurt so much. At my SSA group they keep telling me it takes time and that I should be patient.

Diane: Your SSA group? Help me out with this one, okay?

Nicole: Survivors of Sexual Abuse.

Diane: Oh, Nicole, I'm so sorry. I had no idea.

Nicole: I didn't know either until about a year ago. Then the memories started trickling in. Soon they started flooding in. Now I'm just so angry! The whole thing makes me so angry! You want to know what really ticks me off? That jerk is still working in the same dance studio. He's probably still molesting girls today!

Diane: Nicole, I realize you know this, but I'll say it anyway: This is really one of those times for drawing close to your Savior.

Nicole: My *Savior?* How can you call Him my *Savior?* He certainly didn't save me when I was 11 years old and crying for help. And He hasn't done what I asked Him to do a few months ago either. That creep who molested me is still free!

53

Diane: You're angry at God for not dealing with the man who hurt you. I can understand that. And God can handle your anger. He's pretty tough, you know.

Nicole: You understand? You're not going to judge me for being mad at God? You really think God is willing to put up with my tirades against Him?

Diane: Definitely. Just look at some of the psalms. Those folks did plenty of complaining.

Nicole: So you can do that?

Diane: Of course. But my question, Diane—and forgive me if this makes you uncomfortable—but my question is, are you still doing it? Do you keep going before God's throne with your anger and with your need for justice against that creep who hurt you?

Nicole: No. I quit asking after a couple of weeks. I figured either I wasn't a good Christian or God wasn't a good father.

Diane: A good Christian pesters her Father. And a good father listens and takes action at just the right time. God does listen. He will take action. I don't know how or when; it may not be until Jesus comes back. But He will take action—sometimes He does so in ways that surprise us. Please keep talking to Him and nagging Him about it.

Let's Talk

1. Injustice and abuses of various kinds are the rule, rather than the exception, in this fallen world of ours. Christians are not exempt from various types of injustice and abuse. How had Nicole dealt with the abuse she had experienced and recently recalled? What healthy steps was she taking? What unhealthy ones?

2. Recently Nicole had quit praying and had quit attending the house of prayer, her church. Why had she done so? It seemed to her that God had not answered her prayer. How did this affect her view of herself as a child of God? her view of God as her Father?

3. What do you think of Diane's approach to Nicole? How should we pray when we're angry with God? Think about prayers for justice. How do they fit with a Christian's responsibility to forgive those who have sinned against him or her?

4. If you were called on to pray with and for Nicole, for what would you pray? On returning home and praying for Nicole on your own, what would you ask God to do? Would you ask God to deal in justice with the man who abused Nicole? Why or why not?

How Long, O Lord?

A Widow's Cry

1. Read **Luke 18:1–5.** According to **verse 1,** why did Jesus tell this parable? What are some reasons we sometimes want to give up and quit praying?

2. Jesus told about a widow seeking justice. Read **Deuteronomy 10:17–18.** Given what Jesus' disciples knew about God's feeling for widows, why was such a scenario appropriate? What does this indicate about the type of prayer Jesus talked about when He urged His disciples to keep praying and not give up?

3. Read the rest of the parable, **Luke 18:6–8.** Jesus says His chosen ones will get _____ . What might be some examples of personal prayers for justice in our own day?

4. At first, what kept the unjust judge from responding to the woman's request? In what ways is God different from the unjust judge?

5. In **verses 7–8** Jesus teaches that God will see that His chosen ones get justice "quickly." At times it may seem to us that God is not quickly answering our prayers for justice. We may even think we are not God's chosen ones. What is wrong with drawing such a conclusion?

The Church's Cry

Read **Revelation 6:9–11.** What do these martyrs ask their Lord? Are they in a good relationship with God? Is their request a just one? Is it a request with which God agrees? God does not give them their request right away, and they continue to cry out to God. What does their persistence demonstrate about their relationship with God? What does God's answer show about His time frame for answering some prayers for justice?

So Long, Rich Man!

1. Read **Luke 16:19–31.** Notice the picture painted in **verses 19–21.** Imagine that you are Lazarus. With your mind's eye look down to the end of your own leg and see the sores up and down it. Now look beyond your toes to the sturdy gate leading to the rich man's luxurious home. Likely Lazarus had prayed for justice. Would Lazarus have always felt like God was just toward him? Reread **verse 25** (spoken to the rich man). Was God in fact just toward Lazarus?

2. Sometimes we see people who are tormented with suffering for much of their lives. Although they and we pray that God would remove their sufferings, they sometimes die before the suffering ends. Such a life and death can appear to be a series of fruitless tragedies. Some would conclude that we have either an empty universe or a deaf God. Jesus was not embarrassed to tell this account in which things only come out alright "in the end." Sometimes God does answer our prayer for justice only after this life is over. Meanwhile, what do we do?

Run Along, Impatience!

1. Reread **Luke 18:1** and **7–8.** Jesus knew that great and painful injustices would sometimes come upon His chosen ones and that they would "cry out to Him day and night." If we quit crying out to Him and give up, what might this mean about our faith? Why do you think Jesus raises the question, "When the Son of Man comes, will He find faith on the earth?" What does this question suggest about the timing of some of God's answers to our prayers for justice?

2. It is important to cry out to God and not give up even when doing so doesn't seem to be "working." Our prayer shows that we have faith that God is still in control of the universe, that He still listens to His chosen ones, that He still cares about their plight, and that He will see that they get justice and quickly. If you wish, share one prayer you quit praying but are now ready to pray again.

3. Recite the following aloud together:

As long as a loved one lives in the clutches of unbelief,
I will keep praying for deliverance and faith, Father.
As long as the innocent suffer and the guilty escape,
I will keep praying for justice and equity, Father.
Though my patience is weak, You are strong to deliver.
Though my faith is tested, You are hearing my cry.
Though I cannot see Your hand at work, I will keep praying, Father.
And You will deliver. This I believe.
You alone are God. This I believe. AMEN.

Venturing Out Together
1. Read or sing *LW* 397 or *TLH* 439.
2. Agree on one or more prayer requests the members of your group will bring to God persistently. Consider the needs of group members, members of your congregation, or individuals or groups in your community.

Lesson 10　Prayers Shaped by the Gospel: Peter and John before the Sanhedrin

Acts 4:1–31

Our Itinerary

In this session we will explore how the facts about the life, death, and resurrection of Jesus help us identify the real context of the conflicts we undergo as believers in Christ. We will also explore how the content of the Gospel message provides shape and direction to our prayers when we suffer these conflicts.

Invited into the Adventure

Keith had stopped by his pastor's study after school on a number of occasions. Usually Keith wanted to talk over plans for upcoming youth events he was helping to lead. But this time Keith closed the study door behind him as he came in. This time Keith was here to get some help for himself.

Pastor: Have a seat, Keith. You look worn out.

Keith: I am. I've about had it with Mrs. O'Neal. I think this time she's gone too far.

Pastor: She teaches social studies at Oakview High, doesn't she?

Keith: Yes, and I've got her this semester for an elective called "Alternatives in Coping."

Pastor: Hmm. That sounds like an interesting course. What is it?

Keith: That's what I've been wondering! Mostly we talk about weird things that have to do with spiritual forces. She's had guests come in who supposedly can read our auras. The last guy said my aura reflects a lot of unresolved hostility and judgment. Mrs. O'Neal took us on a field trip to this Hindu temple where we heard this big speech about how all peoples and all religions are really one; enlightened people don't think of their religion as the only right path. We do meditation exercises where we learn to "empty our minds of all content."

I'm not sure my GPA can handle this. My parents say that if I don't qualify for some scholarships, college is out of the question.

Pastor: Do you think Mrs. O'Neal's beliefs might affect your grade for the class?

Keith: That's already happening! She gave us a test with a bunch of scenarios of people with problems; we had to help them learn how to cope. In all of my answers I told them about Jesus dying for their sins and about repenting and believing in Jesus. I suggested that they ask for His help.

Mrs. O'Neal says I've closed my mind to all the valuable things she has taught us. My answers show that I haven't learned a thing! She said she gave me a C instead of an F because she could tell I am "psychically challenged" on account of my "narrow upbringing." What am I supposed to do? It's tempting to just play along. I know what she wants to hear.

Pastor: First of all, Keith, don't worry about the college tuition money. One way or another your future is in good hands. Our Lord will provide you with whatever you need to do His will. Also, I think we'll want to bring this thing to the attention of the school administration—maybe even the school board. I'll help with that. But to start with, Keith, let's pray about this situation. I know you've been praying already, but let's pray together.

Heavenly Father, You sent Your Son Jesus into human flesh as the light of the world. He shined in the darkness, but the darkness didn't comprehend Him. He came to His own people, but His own people didn't receive Him. He was rejected, persecuted, and crucified. By His death He destroyed death. Then He rose again from the dead. We pray, help Your son and servant Keith to stand firm in this battle. Help him continue to shine the light of Your Word even when he may suffer losses. Give him boldness, Lord. We pray this in Jesus' name. Amen.

Let's Talk

1. What appear to be some of Mrs. O'Neal's beliefs and practices? What do you think Keith finds objectionable about them?

2. Keith expressed his faith in the written examination he took for Mrs. O'Neal's class. What beliefs does Keith hold dear?

3. If you were in Keith's situation and were worried about grades and scholarships, how might you handle the course work in this class? What is the cost of discipleship for Keith as he makes a clear Christian testimony in this class?

4. Examine the content of the pastor's prayer. How might this prayer have helped Keith? What parts of this prayer could you see yourself saying? How might you have prayed differently?

5. Keith's pastor asks God to give Keith boldness. If you were Keith's mother or father, how would you feel about this request?

The Cross: Conflict for Power

1. Read **Acts 4:1–7.** The Sadducees rejected the doctrine of the resurrection. What about the apostles' teaching disturbed them and the others? Mrs. O'Neal seems to think that religious groups with differing beliefs can join together as one. Read **John 14:6.** What Christian teachings would unbelievers find objectionable today?

2. Notice the parties mentioned in **verse 5.** These are the same groups who tried Jesus and accused Him before Pilate (**Luke 22:66–23:25**). According to **John 11:45–48,** what motivated this?

3. Peter and John were teaching that God had raised Jesus from the dead (**Acts 3:15**). Why would these religious leaders have feared and hated that teaching?

4. Read **Acts 4:8–12.** Peter does not avoid the "sticky issue" of Jesus' crucifixion and resurrection. What statement does Peter make that is controversial to this very day (**verse 12**)? What sorts of judgments are brought against Christians for their adherence to the truth stated here by St. Peter?

5. Read **Acts 4:13–22.** When we experience peer pressure that tries to discourage us from telling others about the death and resurrection of Jesus, what would Peter tell us? (See **Acts 5:29** also.).

The Cross: Context for Prayer

1. Read **Acts 4:23–31.** Some people think doctrine is the hard, cold, dry stuff of heavy and dusty old books. They may also think that healthy, energetic prayer avoids doctrine too and that it is made of warmer, cozier, softer stuff. In these verses we see how the early church prayed. Match the verse numbers with the doctrine by which and with which these early Christians prayed.

____ **verse 24**   **a.** The Holy Spirit speaks in the Scriptures.

____ **verse 25**   **b.** God is the Creator of the world.

____ **verse 26**   **c.** Jesus is the Anointed One, the Christ.

____ **verse 27**   **d.** God planned Jesus' crucifixion beforehand.

____ **verse 28**   **e.** The Old Testament predicted that Jesus, the Anointed One, would be opposed and persecuted.

2. Look over the above list of teachings the believers recalled as they prayed. If you were in their situation, which teaching would be of greatest comfort to you? Why? How would that teaching help you pray with confident faith?

3. In our worship services we usually hear the Word of God read and we hear the Gospel preached before we do the bulk of our praying. Why do you think the church prays in this way? (Read **James 1:6–7** and **Romans 10:17.**)

4. Reread **Acts 4:29–30.** For what did the believers ask God? For what might you have expected them to ask? Given the context, what purpose do they seem to have in mind for the miracles they request? Read **Matthew 12:39** and **Luke 10:17–20.** As a rule, what did Jesus teach His disciples about seeking miraculous signs? According to **Acts 4:31,** how did God respond to their prayer?

The Cross: Content to Proclaim

1. God gave the disciples the boldness for which they prayed, and they again proclaimed the Gospel. Read **Acts 5:29–32.** What was the content of their proclamation?

2. Read **1 Corinthians 2:2** and **15:1–4.** How does St. Paul summarize the entire Gospel message?

3. Jesus taught us to pray in His name. We often end our prayers with these words: In Jesus' name. Amen.

What we proclaim and how we pray are identical. If this Good News about Jesus' death and resurrection has no place in our prayers, it likely doesn't show up much in our witnessing and teaching either. *In Jesus' name. Amen* only "works" when we pray those words in faith. Mature Christian faith retains the importance of the elementary teachings of the death and resurrection of Jesus. Without those basic beliefs there is no faith. There is no prayer. There is no life with God.

In what ways can meditating on the death and resurrection of Jesus and praying with them in mind help us when we are

a. suffering with guilt over our sins?

b. suffering rejection because of our Christian convictions?

c. suffering from the accusations of Satan?

d. struggling with temptation?

e. saddened by evil, pain, or disease in the world?

Venturing Out Together
1. Read or sing *LW* 381 or *TLH* 409.
2. Develop "prayer pacts" in pairs or small clusters within your study group. Make commitments to pray with and for one another and for needs of friends of cluster members. Possibly set times when cluster members will meet together to discuss their prayer lives.